NEGOTIATION (TECHNIQUES)

THE FUNDAMENTAL PRINCIPLES

Dr Philippe Massol
https://www.linkedin.com/in/philippemassol/

SmartOwl

TABLE OF CONTENTS

You have to negotiate and it's sometimes difficult?
Do you want to improve your negotiation techniques?
Your management puts pressure on you and you don't know how to approach negotiations that can be complex?

The books you have read are too complex, too thick: there is too much information and you are lost?

This book is for you: it will save you a lot of time and energy because you will learn how to negotiate in an environment where uncertainty and irrational behavior may also complicate your task, without getting lost in a multitude of details and subtleties that will be impossible for you to master in the field.

- How do you prepare for a negotiation?
- What proposal to make at the opening of a negotiation?
- How to set an objective?
- What are the possible strategies and tactics?
- What techniques should be used to move forward in the negotiation?
- How to conduct a negotiation?

1

PREPARING FOR THE NEGOTIATION

1.1 WHAT IS NEGOTIATION?

What is negotiation? It is a way of reaching an agreement in a conflict situation between two people or two companies that results in each negotiator getting something that they feel is fair.
If negotiation were based only on rational things, perhaps it would not be so complex, but today's economy and business world has become complex, and there are many uncertainties. At the same time, with the help of internationalization, competition and commercial pressure are increasing. The rational part of negotiations has lost space and uncertainty and the unknown are increasingly present in negotiations. Non-rational factors are also at work:

- the human and relational factor, which is difficult to transcribe into a standard procedure.
- an abandonment of the long-term in favor of the short term: indeed, the short term is increasingly favored because of the pressure felt by companies, and certain negotiation practices are aggressive and dishonest, even if this is to the detriment of the long-term.
- Finally, some companies do not hesitate to use threats or to lie during negotiations.

Issue pressure, time pressure and questionable negotiating tactics are among the most common reasons that diminish the effectiveness of negotiations.
For example, it is not really possible to anticipate what will happen during a negotiation, which is why it is necessary to prepare for it, and to learn to master negotiation techniques in order to obtain maximum value from it.
Of course, the techniques used by companies are also applicable by everyone in their daily life.

1.2 GAINING CONFIDENCE IN YOUR ABILITY TO NEGOTIATE

Negotiation requires practice, but also skills and knowledge that can be acquired. This knowledge will help you gain confidence. Four important things will help you when you are faced with a difficult negotiation for the first time:

Firstly, you will be more confident if you learn and know the basic negotiation strategies, tactics and techniques, as this will be a kind of knowledge base on which you will be able to build in order to move forward in the negotiation. You will be able to distinguish the objective of the issue, foresee counterparts, and you will know what to expect from the other side.

The second thing to do to gain confidence is to learn about the other side. Who are the people you are going to meet? Don't hesitate to search on Google, LinkedIn, or even search their names on YouTube. Try to determine their character, personal activities. If your interviewer(s) are sportsmen and women and you are also sportsmen and women, you have a common subject that you can discuss before starting the negotiation.

The third point that should reassure you before a negotiation is preparation. Going off on an improvisation will not work for you and you have to build and prepare for the upcoming negotiation. You need to know what elements you are going to hide from your opponent, what elements you are going to put forward, you need to have already prepared all the counterparts: that is to say, all the elements on which you are ready to give up some weight in order to get something in return, and you need to have evaluated the counterparts you could demand from your opponent.

Finally, the fourth point will not help you directly to gain self-confidence, but will make the negotiation easier: it consists in giving up your ego. Indeed, ego may be important for self-confidence, but it can become an obstacle in negotiation, because if your ego is highly developed, you will want to impose yourself rather than get the maximum from the other negotiator. On the other hand, too big an ego will make tense negotiations difficult for you, because you will take failures personally: negotiation is only a game, sometimes with zero sums, sometimes with negative sums and sometimes with positive sums.

So, to improve your confidence, forget your ego, know the basic techniques of negotiation, find out about your opponent and prepare your negotiation even if you know that some of it will have to be improvised.

1.3 THE MOTIVATIONS OF BOTH NEGOCIATOTRS ARE ALWAYS MORE COMPLEX THAN THEY APPEAR TO BE

When you start a negotiation, it is not always easy to understand each other's motivations.
Indeed, motivations are usually not told, because a negotiator who would give his or her real motivation becomes more vulnerable to an malicious interlocutor. It is therefore to protect oneself that the real motivations are hidden.
To try to understand how to position oneself in this sometimes opaque game, it is necessary to understand that the initial offer, the stake and the objective are three very distinct things, and only two of them being negotiable.

The first thing is the **initial offer**, which is what the other side is asking for. Consider that this initial demand does not necessarily correspond to the real motivations. At least it has the advantage of being clear and setting a framework from the outset. And it is around this demand that the beginning of the negotiation will be structured.

The second thing is the **objective**. This is what the other side hopes to achieve, and what you really hope to achieve: and it is often less ambitious than the initial offer. In fact, in practice it is always less ambitious than the original offer, because the original offer includes a margin for negotiation. In the objective, it is possible to incorporate any gain, and not only money: it may be to shorten or extend delivery times, obtain better working conditions or even just impose a power struggle to be respected.

These first two points, the **initial offer** and the **objective**, are both negotiable. However, the third point is completely non-negotiable: the **issue at stake**.
The issue is the fundamental need that the other side wants to satisfy in the negotiation, and it is usually not easy to identify.
For example, if the buyer of a business asks for a 10% discount, that is his or her starting offer. He is actually hoping to get a 5% reduction (that is his target), but his issue may be to keep the supplier at all costs, even if he gets nothing. This last point is the issue. Or, conversely, his stake is to get rid of the supplier if he does not bend on everything, in which case he will be uncompromising during the negotiation and will not give in on anything, almost hoping that the supplier will refuse his proposals, in order to get rid of him, which will allow him to shift the blame for the failure of the business relationship onto the supplier.
What is interesting is that the issue at stake is sometimes at odds with the interest of the person negotiating. For example, a salesperson is offended because he feels that he is being treated

badly by a customer. His challenge is to be respected and treated as an equal, but when he cannot get the respect he feels he is owed, he leaves the meeting angry and upset and eventually loses the contract.

Now let's look at how to identify the objective and what is at stake.

The **objective** is the answer to the following question: "What is my interlocutor reasonably seeking to achieve in this negotiation?" For example: to obtain a 5% reduction on the total order.

The stake is the answer to the following question: "What really motivates my interlocutor and what need does he or she seek to satisfy?" Note that sometimes you may not be aware of your own stake! This shows that you have not properly analyzed the situation. If you are aware of your own stake, it will be easier for you to negotiate.

In conclusion, make a clear distinction between the initial offer, the objective and the stake. The stake is the only thing that is non-negotiable, and if you can understand what is at stake, it will be easier for you to find points of support for negotiation.

1.4 ANALYZE AND QUANTIFY THE POWER RATIO

In order to conduct your negotiation properly, you will need to identify the counterparts that you can give up to the other negotiator to get something, but you also need to have a clear idea of the balance of power between the two parties.

List all the elements, i.e. all the points, that will be addressed in the negotiation, and for each of the factors, ask yourself if it is:

- very important,
- important
- or somewhat important for you in the negotiation.

You will assign the weighting of 3 for what is very important, 2 for what is important and 1 for what is fairly important. When I say important: it is for you, but you must also consider what is important for the other negotiator.

	weighting
Delivery time	1
Price	3
Dependence on the opponent	2
Negotiation Point 4	2
Negotiation Point 5	3

Then, you give a score of -1.5 -1. 0 +1 or +1.5 depending on a balance of power in the opponent's favor (very unbalanced or not), a tie, or a balance of power in your favor (very unbalanced or not).

	weighting	Force ratio (-1.5 to + 1.5)
Delivery time	1	-1
Price	3	-1
Dependence on the opponent	2	+1
Negotiation Point 4	2	0
Negotiation Point 5	3	-1

Then calculate the weighted score for each trading point: multiply the weighting by the score. Then, simply add the weighted scores, and divide them by the total of the weights.
You will then obtain a score between -1.5 and +1.5, which will give you the strength ratio of the negotiation.

	weighting	Force ratio (-1.5 to + 1.5)		
Delivery time	1	-1	-1	POWER BALANCE Score between -1.5 and +1.5
Price	3	-1	-3	
Dependence on the opponent	2	+1	+2	
Negotiation Point 4	2	0	0	
Negotiation Point 5	3	-1	-3	
Delivery time	11		-5	-0.45

For example, if you have a score of -0.45, this means that your interviewer has a balance of power in his or her favor, without being strongly dominant.

Analyzing and quantifying the balance of power is not easy, because it takes time and requires thinking about what is at stake in each other's power relationships, knowing that you will not always have the information. But this time spent analyze the situation can give you keys for future negotiations.

1.5 FIND A FOCAL POINT

Negotiations are more or less difficult, but if you are going to face difficult negotiations, it is necessary to find a point of convergence, that is to say a common objective, on which to build the negotiation.
Without this, it will be difficult to move forward, since the objectives and issues are usually different. This may lead to behavior that will not move the negotiation forward:

- Firstly, each holds its position firmly in the hope that the other will give in, which will deteriorate the relationship.
- Second, pressure and threats are used by one to make the other bend.
- Third, one negotiator agrees to give in on everything so as not to break up the relationship, but this will damage the relationship in the long run.

So there has to be a point of convergence, and that point of convergence has to be beneficial to both parties: everybody has to win. There can't be only one winner, because the other negotiator will feel aggrieved. Moreover, this point of convergence may possibly conflict with each negotiator's objectives, but never with each negotiator's stakes, since what is at stake is the underlying motivation.

When the stakes are displayed or obvious, it is much easier to find a point of convergence, than if the negotiation begins without any information. It will then be necessary to try to understand what is at stake for the opposing negotiator by trying to obtain as much information as possible.
For example, suppose there is a conflict between employees, who are asking for a raise, and the management of a company that does not want to grant it. Rather than confronting each other in a war of positions that will lead to nothing, we create a point of convergence that can be: "the economic health of the company".

Once you have identified a possible point of convergence, you have to express it in order to get it accepted. This will result in a sentence such as:
—Hello, thank you for agreeing to come to this meeting. Before we begin, I think it's important that we share an essential element in this negotiation: we want to conduct negotiations that will result in any case in maintaining the economic health of our company and not jeopardize its survival. Do we all agree on this particular point?

Finally, this point of convergence must be accepted by the opposing negotiator: a simple "Yes, we agree" is sufficient. Once accepted, this point of convergence will become a sort of umpire for future negotiations.

This point of convergence is of course used for company negotiations, but it is also something you can use in everyday life. For example, in the case of difficult divorces, a point of convergence can be: "We disagree on many points, however, do we agree that whatever decisions are made, they should be made for the benefit of the children?"
In this case, the point of convergence will be the benefit that children can derive from the different decisions that can be made.

1.6 WHY CAN A FOCAL POINT BE REFUSED?

If a point of convergence is accepted in a negotiation, this facilitates future discussions, but sometimes this point of convergence can be refused. There are several possible reasons for this:

1. Firstly: the convergence point is refused out of simple mistrust of the opposing negotiator, considering that the convergence point is a trap (which may in fact be the case).
2. Secondly: the point of convergence is unsuitable (for example, the management of a company in difficulty proposes a point of convergence on the financial survival of the company, but the main customer who comes to negotiate the rates replies: "I understand your point of view, but you are one of our many suppliers and we are not concerned about the economic health of your company, or even its long-term survival, we just want to discuss the terms and rates for the next six months."
3. Thirdly: there is a blindness to reality that does not allow us to understand the point of convergence. For example, a company's sales management proposes a point of convergence on the financial survival of the

company in relation to its biggest customer, but the customer replies: "What are you talking about? We know that your company is doing very well and has no financial problems, so don't try to confuse us." In this case, the major customer has a false view of what is happening with his supplier. It will then be necessary to use pedagogy to explain the facts.

4. Fourth: the opposing negotiator just wants to oppose to prove its strength. For example, with regard to his image, a rapper may sometimes have more to gain by getting into a conflict with another rapper over a contract problem with a record company than by resolving the problems through peaceful negotiation, as this could make him look "weak". In this case, the issue is to "prove his virulence and display a violent facade", and the focal point cannot oppose this issue. It will be necessary to find a point of convergence that respects the rapper's issue.

In any case, if the point of convergence has been refused, do not open negotiations. Try to understand why it has been refused, and in particular, try to understand whether or not it opposes the opposing side's issue. If this is the case, you will have to find another point of convergence that is compatible with what is at stake for everyone.

If you feel that the point of convergence that has been refused is compatible with both parties' stakes, there is mistrust or the opposing negotiator has not fully understood your proposal for a point of convergence. This will require you to do some pedagogy to explain and present the facts before reformulating the point of convergence differently so that it is accepted.

In conclusion, when you have difficult negotiations to conduct, look for a point of convergence and do not start negotiating until it has been accepted.

1.7 THE OPENING OFFER

When you first enter into a negotiation with someone, you're probably going to discuss about various things, a kind of preamble to the negotiation. Then you're going to have one or the other negotiator make a proposal.
Ideally, wait until the other side makes their proposal, because you will learn useful information.
First, maybe you'll get some good news: they're selling for less than you think, or they're buying for more than you think.
Second, if you make the opening offer first, if you sell, the price you offer may be lower than what the other side was willing to pay. If you are the buyer: if you say how much you are willing to pay, the price may be higher than they expected and your interlocutor will immediately raise his or her rate.

On the other hand, letting the other negotiator open allows you to bounce back on their offer: if you sell and they give a higher budget than expected, you raise your price. And if you buy and they offer you a lower price than you expected, you will be able to buy at a lower price.
So let your contact person make his opening offer, because there is always the possibility of a good surprise. Finally, if there is no pleasant surprise, you will know where you stand.

But what if the other side asks you to open first?
Try to kick in at least once. I'll show you how it can happen, both for buying and selling. Imagine the scene: you're trying to sell a formation and want to avoid giving a price. Your interlocutor starts:

- I'm looking for someone who does telephone sales training to train managers in Morocco, and I've seen videos of you on social networks, would you be interested?
- Yes, of course, with pleasure.

- In fact, I'll need to get an idea of the price pretty quickly: we would need two days of training. How much would it cost?
- Well, it would depend very much on what you want. It depends on the number of participants, the period and your objectives, as there might be some extra preparation to be expected. Do you already have a budget for this?
- No, we don't have a specific budget.
- But maybe you have at least a fork, because that will allow me to see what is doable and what is not...

The only goal here is to get a budget from your contact person and avoid giving your price. This logic works both orally and in writing.
If you manage to get the opposing negotiator to open up about their offer, the negotiation is nonetheless over, because in the vast majority of cases, your interlocutor will lie: lie directly or by omission, about what they really want, their motivation and what is at stake. Indeed, information is an important issue and a negotiator will want to keep information secret in order to take advantage of it during the negotiation. Often, moreover, the offer of openness is greater than what the opposing negotiator really wants: it is a way of testing the ground by testing the reaction of the interlocutor and evaluating his combativeness. For example, if an opening offer is unacceptable and the opposing negotiator does not immediately leave the negotiation and instead tries to reason with his interlocutor, this shows his determination to reach an agreement (this also allows pressure to be applied).

When faced with an unacceptable offer of openness, and this is obvious, verbalise it and rely on unquestionable factual elements. For example, say:
"Today, Forrester Research's study of products in this category shows that all competitors' prices are the same and the margin

is 5%. You're asking for a 20% discount on our product. That's a far cry from market prices and I'm not going to get that level of discount."

This will allow the negotiation to progress more quickly, but if the other negotiator is stubborn, leave the negotiation.

Thus, always try to let your interlocutor make his or her opening offer before you and remember that in most cases, the opening offer will be distorted, since everyone has an interest in hiding his or her objectives and real stakes.

2

NEGOTIATION STRATEGIES AND TACTICS

2.1 THE THREE NEGOTIATION STRATEGIES

During a negotiation, a distinction must be made between strategy, tactics and negotiation techniques. What is the difference between these three notions?

1. Strategy consists in determining the general issue at stake in the negotiation: what is at stake in general terms. This is the final objective to be achieved once we are out of the negotiation.
2. Tactics is the way in which we will conduct the negotiation.
3. And a negotiation technique is a trick to convince your interlocutor.

Let's start by defining the negotiation strategy. There are several of them and we will start with two strategies which, philosophically, are not really negotiation strategies.

First strategy, **intransigence**. You hold your initial position without ever backing down on anything and until the other side agrees: this is the method used by Prime Minister Margaret Thatcher in England against the strikers. The aim is to make the other side bend under pressure: either the other side accepts the proposal or there is no agreement. Either the balance of power is very much in favor of whoever leads this strategy and it can work, or the forces are balanced and, unless there is a stroke of luck, it is unlikely to succeed.

Second strategy: **systematic concession**s. This is another strategy which consists of accepting the demands of the other side, usually without asking for anything in return. You can imagine that this strategy is only followed when we are subjected to a balance of power that is very much to our disadvantage. Again, this is not really negotiation: you accept everything.

Let's now look at the main types of negotiation strategies: competitive, cooperative or semi-cooperative negotiations.

Competition is the most common mode of negotiation: there will be a winner and a loser. There are several reasons for choosing competition:

- It is the default negotiation mode, because it corresponds to the natural psychological functioning of humans, which is usually rather possessive, aggressive and violent.
- When one of the parties has a balance of power in his favor, he will get more through competitive negotiation.
- When one negotiator has already entered a competition, the opposite negotiator will also enter a competition to balance the balance of power.

This explains the success of the competition logic: each time one of the parties has more bargaining power, it chooses the competition, forcing the other negotiator to do the same. For example, faced with a large number of potential suppliers, mass distribution can afford to choose a competitive mode of negotiation systematically, because it will always be a winner. The power is so much in favor of the mass retailer that it can afford open threats: "you lower your prices by 10% or we will deregister all your products". However, it cannot afford this strategy with a supplier whose products are difficult to circumvent.

In contrast to competition, cooperation is a common long-term strategy to create trust. It is a strategy in which the gains will be shared. For this, each negotiator must find that the agreement that will be signed is fair and honest. It is the least profitable strategy in financial terms, but it is useful when the objective of both parties is to create a long-term relationship. For example, it is cooperative when two companies sign a partnership to fight aggressive competitors, or when ethics is an important part of doing business.

Finally, semi-cooperation is dictated by a principle of reality: few people really want to cooperate. Semi-cooperation consists in creating transitional cooperation to take advantage of opportunities or an environment favorable to the creation of value. This type of negotiation generally starts as a classic competitive negotiation, but, arriving at a dead-end negotiation, the two parties to the negotiation find common ground on a cooperative mode for a given issue. This will not prevent a return to a competitive mode of negotiation for another negotiation.

There are variants of semi-cooperative negotiation, depending on whether one or the other negotiator just pretends to want to cooperate for short-term gain or even when one negotiator doubts the sincerity of the other from the outset. For example, two companies agree to share a territory commercially: eastern France for one, western France for the other, but one of the two companies has in fact lied and is secretly looking for customers in the area that is not its own.

Finally, **semi-cooperation** is a type of strategy that follows a competition that does not succeed when the protagonists want to find a solution, because there is a common goal, for example, to fight against very aggressive competitors.
Semi-cooperation works best when both parties have balanced power. One of the factors that can help to stay in this semi-cooperative mode is to define, express and make the parties accept a point of convergence between the parties, and this point of convergence will be recalled when it is felt that negotiation in a "competition" strategy could appear.

In general, competition is the default negotiation strategy. If you want to create positive long-term relationships, perhaps at the expense of the short term, you may want to try the cooperative strategy.

2.2 THE TACTIC OF POINT-BY-POINT NEGOTIATION

Once the negotiation strategy has been chosen: competition, cooperation or semi-cooperation, it will be necessary to choose one of the two negotiation tactics. The negotiation tactic consists of identifying the points that will have to be negotiated and how they will be negotiated. There are only two possibilities: either one negotiates point by point, or one negotiates comprehensively, taking all the points to be negotiated as a whole.

Point-by-point negotiation involves negotiating each point one after the other, and only moving on to the next negotiating point when the previous negotiating point has been agreed to by everyone. Thus, since each point is dealt with separately from the others, there is no plan to return to it in further negotiations since the point is taken for granted.
Point by point has the advantage of being able to move forward fairly quickly, as a complex situation is broken down into several simpler points that can be negotiated separately.

Moreover, when you decide to conduct a point-by-point negotiation, you will be able to benefit from the psychological effect of persevering with the decision. This effect allows you to commit your interlocutors to making decisions before you know what it will really cost them and makes it difficult for them to go back.
Let's see how decision perseveration works. This was illustrated experimentally on a beach in an experiment

described by Robert-Vincent Joule in his 2002 book "petit traité de manipulation".

Imagine, we are on the beach and an experimenter wants to understand how the people around him will react if an accomplice comes to steal his bag. He then tests two situations.

In the first one, he addresses his beach neighbour and asks him:

—Do you mind keeping my bag, I have to go away for five minutes, and I'll be back?

In the second, since he does not want the mere fact of talking to someone to change his behavior, he asks the guinea pigs if they have a light.

We then look at what happens when an accomplice comes to steal the bag. In the case where the experimenter has asked for fire, 20% of the people will intervene to prevent the person from stealing the bag, while in the case where the person has been asked to "keep the bag", 95% of the people will intervene.

What is interesting is that when the question is asked, "Do you mind keeping my bag", the person doesn't imagine for a second that someone is going to steal it. You can imagine that if they thought somebody was going to steal the bag, they would never have agreed to keep it, and if the person being tested had thought that somebody was actually going to steal the bag, they would have said, "Sorry, I can't take that responsibility because there are too many thefts on this beach."

So, by the time the person decides to accept to keep the bag, they are 100% sure that it will never be stolen! This does not prevent them from intervening during the theft when they would not have wanted to do so a priori. The phenomenon I have just described to you is called "decision perseveration". What happens is that people adhere more to the choice they made at the beginning, rather than to the reasons that made that choice. It is a bit like forgetting the reasons for one's decision in the first place, and continuing by default to maintain one's decision even if reality has changed and one would not have made the same choice under those conditions.

In negotiation, this effect of persevering with the decision is the key psychological point when you engage in a point-by-point negotiation, because your interlocutor accepts certain points in the negotiation without yet knowing what the future points will really cost him or her.

I will call this the priming technique. Decisions are made without the person knowing the real cost. In fact, it's a little more subtile than that. There are actually three steps in this priming process:

1. First step: you get the other side to decide when they don't yet see what's at stake in the negotiation.
2. Second step: the opposing negotiator discovers that his decision is not as advantageous as that.
3. Step Three: The opposing negotiator is asked whether or not they will maintain their decision. We can say:—We've been negotiating for a long time and have already agreed on prices. It seems that the volumes purchased are less than you imagined, and perhaps that seems less interesting to you. Of course, we can start the whole negotiation all over again, and we are ready to do so. What do you want to do to each other?

When the negotiator is not very experienced and does not know the principle of priming, the percentage of acceptance will be higher than it would have been if the price and volume information had been given from the start.

It is important to obtain approval in a context of freedom, because it is enough for your interlocutor to feel pressured and trapped, for him to decide to question the different points negotiated, or to decide to transform the negotiation point by point into a global negotiation, and ask to start from scratch.

2.3 THE TWO LOGIC OF POINT-BY-POINT NEGOTIATION

When you have chosen to negotiate point by point, you have two possible choices for ranking points you negotiate against each other: go from the easiest point to negotiate to the hardest point, or the other way around.

When you go from the easiest to the hardest point, it allows you to move forward quickly and it allows you to reach consensus: it creates a rather positive atmosphere if it happens those first steps. Once you get to the difficult point to negotiate, that's the only point left to resolve and the negotiation is over. This helps to motivate everyone to make efforts, because if the parties do not reach an agreement, all agreements on the previous points are cancelled and you have to start from scratch. This is a good way to do it when you have a lot of issues to negotiate and a lot of time.

When you go from the most difficult point to negotiate to the easy points, it can be disadvantageous in the short term because it can strain relationships, but if the most difficult point of negotiation is reached and an agreement is reached, the secondary points will be easier to finalize. This is a good way to go if you have very little time, and you don't have the opportunity to spend time discussing side issues when the main issue has not yet been addressed.

Whichever logic you choose, point-by-point negotiation has three major drawbacks:

- First, the parties must agree on each point.
- Second, a single point of disagreement can stop the negotiation process.

- Third, if one of the parties does not want to address two points separately, but wants to link them together, the negotiation switches to an overall negotiation. For example, if your supplier says, "we agreed to a significant discount on our rates in our first point during the negotiation, but now that we're talking about quantities, I realize that volumes will be low. At this level of volume, I will not be able to maintain the price we agreed to, because there is obviously a link between the prices we give and the volumes purchased. "The point-by-point technique didn't work: you wanted to get both a low price and low volumes, but the other side realized this and doesn't want to accept it. In this case, the negotiation switches to a global negotiation tactic, whether it is intended or not.

2.4 GLOBAL NEGOTIATION AND ITS TWO LOGIC

The Global Trading Tactic is the default trading mode, as it automatically weights the gains and losses of each of the points traded for a better balance.

The advantage of global trading is that it is possible to link all the points in a set that will allow you to obtain counterparts since a gain on one point can be offset by a loss on another point, and vice versa.
On the other hand, the disadvantage is that because all points are linked, the questioning of individual points and the permanent rebalancing of gains and losses can make the negotiation last a very long time, as each negotiator can constantly question what has been agreed upon. On the other hand, since everything is constantly changing in the balance of

gains and losses on the different points, it is necessary to be very focused and to note all the details of the negotiation to know exactly where one stands.

As with point-by-point negotiation, there are three ways to manage the overall negotiation:

- First way: by first tackling the simplest points to negotiate and then the most complex ones,
- Second way: the opposite, i.e. starting with the most difficult points to finish with the simplest ones.
- Finally, third way, a combination of the two approaches. You start with the most difficult point. You never know, maybe there will be good news and the negotiation will be simple. And if you realize that there is a lot of friction on the difficult point, you propose to drop the difficult point to come back to it later and you start with the easiest points. This allows you to move forward on some points, while knowing what might be a problem later on the hardest point(s).

So, to sum up, you have two possible negotiation tactics: point by point negotiation or global negotiation, and for each of them you have to choose whether you want to go from the hardest points to the hardest points or the other way around, without closing the possibility to start with the hard point to test the opposite side and move immediately to the easier points in case of resistance.

3

NEGOTIATION TECHNIQUES

3.1 INFORMING CORRECTLY

Negotiation techniques are the way you will manage the face-to-face interaction to achieve a very short-term result. There are many of them and we will look at the most common techniques. Knowing them will help you to negotiate better, but it will also give you a better understanding of what the other side is doing when they are negotiating with you.

One category of negotiation techniques is factual information: it is about proving something factually to show the other side that your proposal is good for everyone and should be accepted.
Ideally, the information you give, in order to be considered factual, should be based on what I call a bibliographic reference, that is, proof of the information you give. For example, you can say:
"a Forrester Group study published last year in December showed industry growth of 12.7%, which will allow you to amortize the royalty cost for our patent in just two years".
However, it is essential to cite an external and recognized source of information, because the trap would be that your interlocutor would question the source of information to reject your proposal.

For example, if you say:
"We did an internal survey last year, and we showed that the industry growth is 12.7%, which will allow you to amortize the royalty cost for our patent in only two years.
The information is not credible because you generate it. All the people you're talking to will have to do is say:
—I find it hard to believe you, we don't have the same numbers. We also did our survey internally and identified a growth potential of only 2%.

In the case of very complex negotiations with several interlocutors, informing correctly may involve taking a roundabout way to inform the negotiator, for example by trying to inform the negotiator through one of his colleagues who seem to think like you. For example, you have identified a member of your interlocutor's team who is fairly permeable to your ideas. During a break at the coffee machine, you give him/her information and try to convince him/her. You then secretly hope that he will tell his team, because if your main negotiating partner trusts this person, the information will have more influence on him than if you give it directly to him. It's kind of a roundabout way of passing on information.

An effective way to try to convince is to show that if there is no agreement, the situation is less good for your interlocutor than if he accepts your proposal, you have to show him the gain. This is a kind of comparison between what his situation would be if he accepted, and what his situation would be if he did not accept.

This negotiation technique works well if you bring a real added value to your interlocutor, because the quasi-scientific proof that you are going to bring could reassure him.

3.2 BE CHARMING

It is interesting to convince with solid arguments. But in a negotiation, human relations and psychology play an important role. Being liked or loved can be as important as arguing well. This is called the sympathy effect.

Sympathy is not only a personal characteristic, it is also a sales and negotiation technique. We can even be more precise: there is a context in which sympathy is more particularly important for success: it is when you negotiate with someone who could work with others than you and when he or she feels that you are replaceable. In this context, your interlocutor will accept things just because he likes you and finds you sympathetic, and he prefers to work with you rather than with other, less sympathetic people!

In sales, this is easy to illustrate: door-to-door sales is a typical example where sympathy will have a lot of influence. Participants in a door-to-door sales meeting some of them already know the salesperson and others will be able to interact at length with the person recommended to them. What is noticeable is that during these meetings, people are usually aware of the buying pressure due to this proximity and the fact that the person selling is sympathetic or liked. Some people manage to overcome this, but many find it difficult to leave a meeting without buying anything, even if they don't need anything. They buy just to please the person they like.

What can make you like someone without too much effort?

1. the tone of your voice should be cheerful and dynamic.
2. you must remember the first and last names of each of your interlocutors
3. you must smile easily
4. Finally, similarity creates sympathy: those who resemble us are sympathetic to us. Whenever the conversation drifts towards a subject that the other negotiator is passionate about and that is not related to the subject of the negotiation, don't hesitate, push them to talk about it, especially if you are interested in it yourself. And if you are an expert on their own passion, don't show too much of your science, allow them to value themselves. Do you swim? What's your specialty? Well, I'm a 200-meter swimmer ... et caetera. Whenever you can, bounce back on things that you personally have in common with the person you're talking to. This classic way of making yourself appreciated is the sales

technique known as foot-in-mouth, which also works in negotiation. It consists of not entering into a negotiating relationship immediately when you meet the other negotiator, but of talking about other, usually trivial subjects, with the aim of creating a personal relationship that will facilitate the interaction with your interlocutor. This technique has been tested and illustrated during a cookie sale for the benefit of a charity association. It is possible to go from 10% to 25% of a purchase by using a foot in the mouth as simple as "how are you today?". The key point is the dialogue between the seller and the person being solicited.

You can find many ways to approach the person you're talking to: in particular, find out about social networks and find out what they like to talk about: talk about swimming to swimming enthusiasts, about classical music to classical music enthusiasts and, in general, try to find personal common ground.

Interestingly, being sympathetic will have an effect even when the person you are talking to is aware that there is pressure to be sympathetic. On the other hand, if there are several people involved in the negotiation, the people on the other side will surely like each other: be sympathetic to everyone and try to create personal relationships with everyone, not necessarily only the decision maker or negotiator.

The next time you enter into a negotiation for the first time, try to find common points with the other negotiator and get them to talk about subjects they are passionate about.

3.3 BE INTERESTING AND CONVINCING WITH STORIES

To charm is not only to be appreciated as a person, it is also to construct a conversation which attracts. And for this, being able to tell interesting stories and anecdotes is an interesting negotiating lever. In order for your anecdotes to correspond to the structure of a convincing story that is easy to remember, you will need to structure your speech in four essential steps:

1) You must begin by describing the reality, i.e. the situation today, in a factual way.
2) Secondly, you must describe the problem encountered by each of the parties. For example, describe why you have to negotiate.
3) Third step: you will describe the consequences of not reaching an agreement. This is an important part of the stories, but it is a part that is often forgotten. This will allow the other side to realize the negative impact of not reaching an agreement.
4) Finally, you will show that by accepting your proposal, everyone wins.

Here is an example that follows the structure of a story:

- Hello, thank you for agreeing to meet me. We've been lowering our prices for the past six months to gain market share over each other. The problem is that we've both been cutting our margins. If we continue like this, we're both going to make less and less money, and maybe we'll even end up working for free by trimming our margins, no matter who wins this trade war. I have no ego in this story, and I don't care who's the strongest, I just want to make as much money as possible, and I think the same goes for you, I guess your goal is to make money and not to say you're the strongest?

- Yes, I do, especially since I'm accountable to my shareholders...
- So we have a common goal, to make money, and it would be suicidal to continue like this. I propose that we divide up the geographical areas and work closely together to maintain the highest possible margins for each other, while protecting our geographical area from the arrival of new competitors. Is that okay in principle?
- Okay, in principle!

Following the structure of a story will save you from having negotiations that go into the wall as in the following example.

- Hello, we've been competing head-on for six months: I suggest that you share the geographical zones with us to stop fighting each other commercially.
- I understand your proposal, but we think we can beat you in every department...
- Still, it would be better for everyone, wouldn't it?
- I'm sorry, but may the best man win.

A story doesn't guarantee anything, but it's often much more persuasive because of its structure:

- Location
- Problem
- Negative consequences if no agreement is reached,
- Win, if we accept your proposal.

These stories, when told well, have the big advantage that they address the reptilian brain of your interlocutor, i.e. his emotional brain. It can be about playing on envy, jealousy, fear or frustration; and these emotions are powerful decision activators.

Thus, beyond the factual information useful for convincing, the way in which you are able to argue may influence your interlocutor, especially if you know how to argue by following the structure of a story. The more you can tell interesting stories that are emotionally appealing to the other person, the more likely it is that you will be able to move the negotiations in your favor.

3.4 BALANCE OF POWER

There are more violent techniques of negotiation, but to do that, you have to be clearly the stronger, and you have to have decided to win one negotiation at the expense of the other.
In principle, you're going to put very strong pressure on the other side.

First possibility: you knock out the other side right from the start. For example, one month before a commercial renegotiation with a very large distributor, a company receives a letter from the latter stating: "we thank you for your collaboration with our company over the last three years: it has been decided to delist all your products for next year. However, we will keep our appointment for next month to explain the reasons for this choice and to allow you to adapt your offer if you have the possibility to do so". If the weight of the distributor in the company's turnover is important, the stakes for the supplier are enormous, and the pressure put on the supplier's sales representative is gigantic: the survival of the company is at stake. It is likely that all future applications will be accepted, regardless of their nature, especially if there is no short-term fallback solution for the supplier.
On the other hand, if the supplier accepts all the conditions that will be imposed at the meeting and signs again with the distributor in question, it is likely that the company's general management will ensure that fallback solutions are found for the following year, in order to reduce the balance of power and to be able to reduce the dependence on large-scale distribution

for their business. Thus, putting very strong pressure on their interlocutor is certainly profitable in the short term, but not necessarily in the long term.

Second possibility: you scare people in a roundabout way.
For example, a major retailer has run a poster campaign aimed at the general public in which it states that it has deregistered this or that well-known branded product because price increases would be too expensive, arguing that it is thus protecting consumers' purchasing power. This a priori advertising campaign aimed at the general public was in fact also aimed at all suppliers, whoever they may be: it conveyed the following message: we can decide to deregister any product at any time without notice. It's a kind of hidden terror policy to make sure that the suppliers behave in their place. Intimidation can also take the form of a personal attack: for example, you negotiate contracts on behalf of your company, and the other side tells you:

- We have offered you something completely honest and acceptable, you make little effort to accept our point of view, and if you continue in your stubbornness, you take responsibility for making our business relationship fail. I am curious to know how the management of your company will react and what consequences your failure will have on your professional future if we do not find a solution.

For example, when there is a great imbalance of power, the strongest can use the balance of power to win a negotiation, but this is not always a good calculation in the very long term.

3.5 MANIPULATION

Less ethical, because they are underhanded or camouflaged, manipulation techniques can be used to try to reach an agreement in your favor. This involves using psychological techniques and changes in perception of reality to get something from the other side.

First manipulation: giving a false objective.
It is a matter of making the interlocutor believe that the most important thing for you is a point that is in reality of little importance, in order to be able to step back on the subject by presenting it as a big concession and having a lot in exchange, when in fact it represents little. For example, you say:

- What matters to me is the delivery time more than the price. It's very important for our internal manufacturing processes. I can't back off on this delivery issue unless you lower the price so that it becomes attractive to us.

This will allow you to let go of the deadline and get a better price, especially if you know that the other negotiator does not have the possibility to shorten the deadline.

The second way to manipulate, which I would advise you not to use, but you should know that it exists: you're lying.
The principle is obvious, you're lying outright. For example, by promising something when you already know you won't keep your word. On the other hand, once the lie is exposed, all trust is broken.

Third way to manipulate: showing disinterest.
This is a great classic in negotiation techniques. For example, if you want to buy something that you think is great and that you love: above all, don't show your interest. Make a jaded face and criticize the product. For example, you can say that you already have two bikes and that you don't need a third one. For a piece of furniture, you can pretend that you're not sure it will fit in

your living room. In any case, don't look enthusiastic and say something in the style:

- I don't really want to buy, but if the price was really good, I might be tempted even if I don't need it.

Showing disinterest also works for selling products or services. For example:

- Honestly, I'm not too motivated to come and do two days of training in four half-days: it makes me lose two days of availability and I have four times the train journey to make. I would prefer to do the training in two consecutive days. Now, let's be honest, it's feasible, but not at the standard fare.

How do you react when in negotiation your interlocutor tries to manipulate you?
Think of it as a negotiation technique. Always imagine that in reality, your interlocutor really wants to reach an agreement and he wants absolutely what you are proposing. If you see it that way, you are less likely to back down.

In any case, these manipulation techniques are ethically questionable, especially lying, which, if discovered, makes you lose all credibility.

3.6 THE TOUCH TECHNIQUE

Among negotiation techniques, the touch technique does not require a single sentence to be pronounced. It is a technique that can only work in face-to-face situations because physical contact must be made.
So what is the technique of touch?
The technique of touching consists of touching, for a second or two, one of the following parts of your interlocutor:

- the shoulder,
- the back,
- forearm

Attention: the handshake doesn't count as it is a usual social contact!

The impact of touch has been tested in various situations, let's see the result it can give in the tests that have been made: the test is made in a shop with fitting rooms. Parts are left on the seat. The people who pass behind pick up these parts. When they come out, the experimenter goes to see them and asks them: "Excuse me, you wouldn't have found any coins that I left on the seat in the fitting room?". The experiment will be conducted in two ways:

1) The control conditions under which we will **not** touch the other person...
2) The test conditions under which the person will be touched

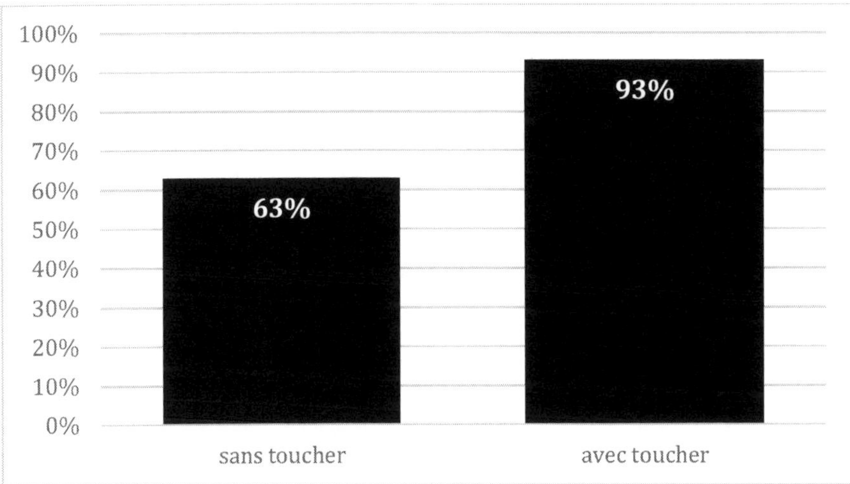

Under controlled conditions, 63% of people will give change that was found in the changing rooms. Under touching conditions, 93% of people will return the change that was found in the changing rooms.

The touch technique has been tested in different contexts and it has been shown that it can influence aesthetic judgements, finding a more pleasant store, finding the staff pleasant or creating a positive mood.

This technique of touch is particularly unintuitive, as it forces one to penetrate the private distance of the interlocutor, which can make one feel uncomfortable: one is afraid that the interlocutor will feel assaulted.

And it is true that the person touched may not like, or be surprised to be touched. Indeed, there are four physical-psychological distances:

- The **intimate** distance of about 50 cm, in which one creates a feeling of intrusion. This is too short a distance for negotiation.
- The **private** distance, which is 20–30 cm longer than the intimate area, i.e. 50–70 or 80 cm. This is the acceptable

distance in a face-to-face standing negotiation with only one interlocutor.

- The **social** distance, which ranges from 70 cm to 3 min 50 s, a distance used for non-personal conversations: for example, you are talking with someone in the street asking for directions.
- The **public** distance: beyond 3 min 50 s, it corresponds to a communication in front of a group: a conference or a training session.

These four distances actually have values that vary with cultures and countries, for example, Anglo-Saxon countries have a much greater intimate and personal distance than Middle Eastern countries. This is where it becomes interesting and surprising! The technique of touch has been tested in different cultures, and it works whether they are cultures with a large private distance or those with a rather short private distance. One hypothesis is that it is precisely the fact of entering the private and intimate distance with one's hand that creates the positive effect of the technique of touch.

In conclusion, if you want to positively influence your interlocutor, and if you have the courage to do so, use the technique of touch. Conversely, if you find that your interlocutor has touched you, it is you who could be influenced by this technique.

4

CONDUCTING THE NEGOTIATION

4.1 LISTING COUNTERPARTS

In a negotiation, you're going to have to give to receive in return. This is the role of counterparts: they allow each of the parties to make concessions in order to get something in return.

Never give without compensation, because what you give without compensation is of no value to the other negotiator. For something to have value, you have to have fought for it.
Beyond being a bargaining chip, consideration is also meant to justify the offers made at the outset. Let me explain: if you agree to concede something without consideration, this shows that your initial offer was exaggerated. Asking for a counterpart allows you to justify your initial offer, which would otherwise be considered overestimated.
On the other hand, if you give something for free, your interviewer will understand that all you have to do is put pressure on yourself to get something more, without having to give anything. You will find yourself in a situation where the person you are talking to is constantly asking you for more concessions.
This is why it is essential to ask for a counterpart every time you give in on a point: each must take a step towards the other.

The rewards can be very varied: money, time, information, visibility. In fact, a counterpart can be anything of value to the other negotiator. In principle, the goal of the game is to give counterparts that have little value to you, and a lot of value to the other negotiator. It is this exchange of counterparts, usually non-monetary, that can move the negotiation forward.

Before trading, you will have to list all the counterparts you can give. But how do you distinguish between what you can afford to give and what you can't? The principle will be quite simple: a counterpart is something that is less valuable to you than to the

other negotiator, which means that you will get more than what you give.
Conversely, you should not give in on items that are more valuable to you than to the other side, because that would mean that you give more than you receive.

You can build a table with four columns:
First column: the possible counterpart, second column: the value for you, third column: the value for the other side. You can add a fourth column in which you write down what you would like to get in exchange for the consideration you give.

Possible counterpart	Value for me	Value for him	What I want in exchange
Delivery delay	*Weak*	*Strong*	*Lower price*
Price	*Very high*	*Middle*	*nothing*
...	...	...	...

Therefore, it is important to prepare the counterparts you will grant before you start a trade, and to rank them according to their value to you and your interlocutor.

4.2 PROPOSING COUNTERPARTS

When you have to make concessions and propose counterparts, it will be necessary to propose it correctly. Moreover, what will be given by each negotiator will obviously depend on the balance of power between the two parties, and you will have to be careful not to make one of the two most common mistakes:

1) First mistake: ask for counterparts whose value is too high for the opposite negotiator in exchange for a concession that you will have to make anyway, because you have no choice, the balance of power not being in your favor.
2) Second mistake: using your counterparts too quickly in order to obtain concessions from the start quickly, only to find yourself later on with no counterpart to give.

How to formulate a request properly? It's better to ask for something **before** offering a counterpart: don't give up a quid and then ask for something. Say:

- If you don't take the parking lot with the apartment, I can lower the price from 151,000 to €130,000.

Rather than saying:

- All right, I'll offer you the apartment for 130,000... But you won't get the parking space with the apartment.

You might get the following answer:

- okay for €130,000, but on the other hand, the apartment is planned with a garage, we want to keep it!

The first version works better simply for reasons of organization in the speech: when you start your sentence with the condition (the "if" at the beginning of the sentence), the person listening to you does not know what you are going to say in the rest of the sentence, but he already knows that there will be a condition, and just behind it, a consequence, which will be your counterpart. This structure has more impact in making it clear that there is a concession to be made in exchange for the consideration you will give.

Finally, it is sometimes necessary to give without any counterpart. But in that case, you have to be able to justify it, even if only symbolically. For example, you can say:

- Since we want to conclude the agreement today and we prefer to favour the commercial relationship between our companies rather than the balance of power and the short term, we have decided to accept the additional 1% price reduction on our products".

Be vigilant in making concessions without compensation: you have to indicate that this is exceptional, because the other side may consider it to be something normal and worthless. Indeed, if you renegotiate in the future with the same interlocutor, you risk having a reply in this style:

- Of course, like last year, you don't charge us for bathroom tile finishes.

In conclusion, be careful to always ask for something in exchange for your concessions and justify at least symbolically a concession without compensation.

4.3 HOW TO APPROACH THE OPPONENT FROM A PSYCHOLOGICAL PERSPECTIVE

A large part of the negotiation is based on the personal relationships between the negotiators. When negotiation becomes tense, as everyone has his or her own objectives and stakes, and everyone thinks he or she is doing the right thing, it is necessary to understand how to approach the negotiation from a psychological point of view. To make your life easier, you will have to accept three things in the relationship with your interlocutor(s):

First, there are no good guys and bad guys, those who are right or wrong. The representative of a Vegan association may argue that you should not consume any product that exploits animals, and the representative of a butcher shop may consider it natural to consume cattle. Everyone has his or her own vision of the world and you must consider that neither one is right: both visions are defensible.

Second: don't judge the people you are negotiating with because you may reduce the chances of resolving conflicts during the negotiation. By judging the person with whom you are negotiating, you will be attributing wishes and objectives that may not be accurate. On the other hand, if something makes the negotiator unsympathetic and hateful to you because of poor behavior at meals together, you may choose conflict over seeking a peaceful solution. Therefore, do not judge people, but focus only on offers.

Third: use non-verbal language to communicate and use your **body position** to put yourself in a winning frame of mind.

Indeed, it has long been known that mood can have an influence on the body. For example, if you're depressed, you'll withdraw into yourself and lower your voice tone while looking down. Researchers have looked at the role that body position can have on mood and whether or not you feel good. To measure this, they looked at the impact of body position on the levels of hormones that control stress and dominance (these hormones are cortisol and testosterone).

What is a dominance position? Alpha dominance positions are the body posture of someone who is very confident and fit: the hands are on either side of the body so that the stomach and chest are exposed. This indicates self-confidence. However, beta positions indicate submission: arms are generally crossed, sometimes with a hunched back, a bit like when you're sitting down to consult your smartphone.

Experimentally, when a person maintains a physical position of dominance for at least two minutes, they feel much less stressed and much more confident: they will see their cortisol drop and their testosterone increase. Testosterone is the hormone associated with dominance, while cortisol is associated with stress resistance. What do we see when we look at primates? Alpha males have high testosterone and low cortisol. And it is better to negotiate by being dominant and a little stressed than the opposite: this will limit aggressive reactions.

Here's what was tested: several people with similar resumes held an alpha position or a beta position of domination for two minutes before a very stressful job interview. This interview was recorded and shown to potential recruiters, who were asked which people they would be most likely to hire. The preferred people were those who held alpha positions, those who held beta positions were not selected. But what led to this? It is not in the content of the speech. It's in the presence they bring to the speech and not in the speech itself.

Thus, the physical position of your body will influence your own behavior to the extent that it will change the perception people have of you. When you are negotiating, you need to show a dynamic and confident image of yourself, so it is in your best interest to maintain as many alpha positions as possible throughout the negotiations.

4.4 TAKING A SEAT AT THE NEGOTIATING TABLE

Imagine: you are going to negotiate a contract and you enter for the first time in the room where your contact person is already settled. You've spotted his place and you're going to have to choose your seat: which chair should you choose for more efficiency?
What I am about to tell you will seem like a tiny detail, but it is important. Indeed, the way you will place yourself in relation to your interlocutor will give the state of mind of the negotiation.

If you stand in front of him, each on his own side of the table, it symbolizes competition, with each one on his own territory: you are in a struggle against each other.

This is a position you had better choose if the bargaining power is in your favor, because you will be able to mark the balance of power in your favor.

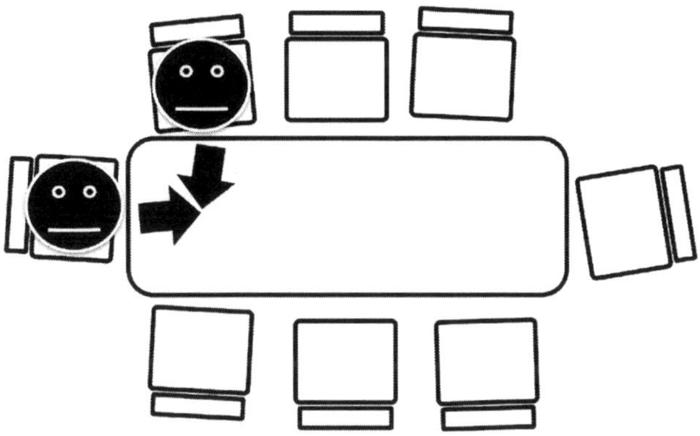

If you stand at a right angle next to your interlocutor, you are in a position that symbolizes cooperation and willingness to listen. The non-verbal aspect of this position indicates to the other negotiator that you want to move forward and make the negotiation a success. Favour this position when you have negotiating power to your disadvantage and you don't know your counterpart very well (or at all).

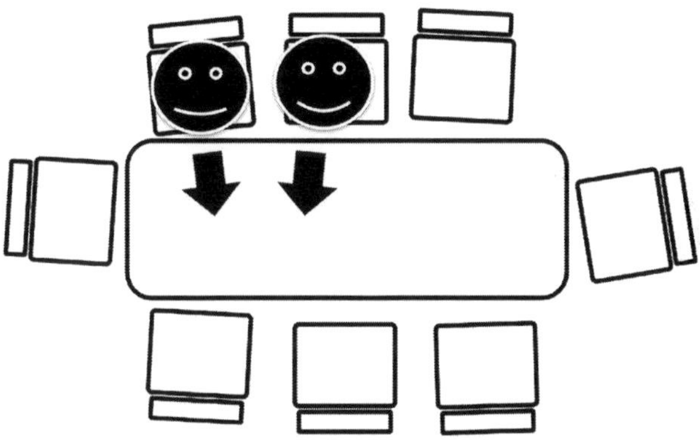

Finally, if you stand next to your interlocutor, it is an even stronger non-verbal signal, because it not only shows that you want to cooperate and make the negotiation successful, but it also shows a certain closeness to your interlocutor. In general, what is said about this position is that you can only do it with a friend or a very good acquaintance. I don't quite agree. It's

certainly difficult to sit next to someone you don't know or know very little about, but I would advise you to use violence and to force yourself to do so.
A few years ago, I was face to face with the training manager of a large company, me in my little chair, him behind his big minister's desk. This is a person I had never met before, but I had spoken to her on the phone, and she was quite nice. During the meeting, at the first opportunity (which was when I had to show documents), I went around the desk and took a chair to sit right next to the person I was talking to. Needless to say, I didn't move any more, I was not to come back face to face! The tone of the conversation, which was rather formal, relaxed and the conversation became much more friendly, as equals.

It is therefore possible to sit next to the other side: you just need a good reason to do so: the simplest reason is to have to show something on paper or on a computer. Use the following sentence:

- I'd have to show you something on this paper if you don't mind.

And you stand up while you say this sentence, and you will put the document and the computer next to the person you are talking to without asking their opinion. You can stand bent over the document next to the person you're talking to, and after a few seconds, as you continue to speak, you sit down on the chair that's there next to them. Once you sit there, don't move!

Be vigilant: the state of mind in which you arrive at a first meeting for a negotiation will influence the choice you will make when choosing your place around the table: if you come with fear in your stomach or if you are very powerful in relation to the other side, you will naturally come face to face. If you are relaxed, you will more easily tend to sit next to the other side. This makes sense.
What is less intuitive is that the physical position you take around a table will influence your morale. If you have fear in

your stomach, but you manage to sit next to the other side, you will soon feel better, and the other side will tend to be less aggressive. The only danger is that someone who wants to play the balance of power in his or her favor will dryly send you back across the table: "Excuse me, please go back across the table!"
In this case, it will cast a chill, but you will have gained from it all the same: firstly, because even if it only worked one time out of three, it is interesting, and secondly, because faced with such an aggressive response from your interlocutor, you now know that he is in an assumed competitive mode of negotiation: he wants to fight, and the negotiation strategy is now clear.

4.5 TIPS AND TRICKS FOR CONDUCTING A NEGOTIATION

Beyond the strategic, tactical and technical aspects of negotiation, there are some tips to know to make your negotiation easier.

First, talk little and listen a lot.
Of course, it is important to know how to express yourself well and be eloquent enough to convince. But above all, it is useful to listen to the other person in order to understand the basis on which you can make progress in the negotiation.
Be careful not to manage a negotiation as you might manage a sales meeting. When you sell something, you propose a product that solves someone's problem, and you show them what it can do for them: the buyer and the seller therefore have a common objective: to solve the buyer's problem.
In negotiations, a priori, you do not have this common objective, and it is therefore in your interest to get your interlocutor to talk to you in order to understand as well as

possible what is his interest, his objective and above all what is at stake.

Secondly: when you speak, try to ask questions.
Indeed, it is the one who asks the most questions that leads the negotiation, because it is the one who will have the most information of the two. This will also mean less talking, and therefore less revealing. Another advantage is that the one who asks questions has more time to think since he or she is listening. For this to work well, it is important to ask open-ended questions, not closed questions. Don't ask:

- Is delivery time important to you?

Instead, ask:

- Why is the delivery time important to you?

Third: Use time as a counterpart
Let's imagine: you have little room for manoeuvre in a negotiation that everyone wants to see succeed. You have a possible solution, but you feel that if you propose it right away, it will be rejected by the other side. So save this solution for the end of the negotiation, so that your solution is seen as the last possible solution, when you knew from the beginning that it would be the only solution.
If you allow the negotiation to last long enough, the other side will have the impression that they have fought for this last solution and it will then be worthwhile, whereas if you had proposed it right away, it would have been rejected. Worse, your solution would have little chance of being accepted at the end of the negotiation because of the psychological phenomenon of persevering with the decision: having already refused this solution at the beginning of the negotiation, the opposing negotiator would find it difficult to accept it later.
Thus, by lengthening the duration of a negotiation, by making it laborious, difficult and exhausting, you create value for a solution that you could have presented from the beginning, but which would then have no value.

Fourth: Make sure that the other side never loses face.
When a negotiation is difficult, colorful words may be exchanged on both sides. As soon as a person gets personally offended, it no longer allows for negotiation, because it becomes a confrontation between individuals. It is certainly very difficult, but try not to have an ego in a negotiation, and focus on the only result. That is why, if one or the other negotiator has to be humiliated, and if you think you are capable of bearing it, it is better that it is you than the other negotiator. In fact, you must try to put yourself in a state of mind where you consider that you are negotiating with a problem and not with a negotiator. What I mean by that is that you have to see your interlocutor as perfectly interchangeable with any other person, so you have to completely ignore emotionally what the interlocutor represents as a person.

4.6 DON'T TRY TO OPPOSE THE OPPONENT

The other side says something you don't agree with. If you simply oppose the opponent, you are pushing the negotiation to a standstill, each side standing in its own position. For example :

- We've developed a video game that makes you want to come back and play it all the time and I hope you'll finance it.
- I've tried it, but compared to the competition, it doesn't really make you want to come back and play it.
- I have ten years of experience in the game, you can trust me, it's going to work very well.
- On the contrary, I think that you have a great risk of failure, because the game is not yet perfected.

- Look, creating games is my job, you're not going to teach me what's addictive and what isn't!
- Maybe not, but I am a game user, and yours is clearly not very addictive.
- You say that because you don't know anything about the industry!

This discussion is getting nowhere, because everyone is trying to counter the other side. If you have to counter-argue, the only solution is to provide indisputable references that prove your interlocutor wrong. Tell yourself that your personal ideas have no importance and little impact in the negotiation. External sources are much more powerful.
Let's take the previous dialogue as an example:

- We've developed a video game that makes you want to come back and play it all the time and I hope you'll finance it.
- I've tried it, but compared to the competition, it doesn't really make you want to come back and play it.
- I have ten years of experience in the game, you can trust me, it's going to work very well.
- As you know, all the scientific literature that deals with game addiction identifies a combination of three factors: the switch, the variable reward, and the commitment of the user or player. In your game, the variable reward lever does not exist. However, there is a synergistic effect of these three factors, and when one of them is missing, the addiction has been proven to collapse exponentially. That's why I think your game remains risky in a market where addiction is important for business development.
- Look, creating games is my job, you're not going to teach me what's addictive and what isn't!
- This is not my intention: on the other hand, could you explain to me how you create addiction without

following the psychological rules described in the scientific literature?

In this case, the discussion is about the content and not the form and this will allow us to move forward in the negotiation rather than having each side stick to their positions. In short, do not try to counter the opposing side unless you have arguments cited by external sources that the opposing side considers reliable. Scientific evidence is usually the strongest evidence you can provide.

4.7 TIPS FOR BETTER LISTENING

Listening is an important skill in negotiation. Here are some tips that will make it easier for you to retrieve information.

Tip #1: **Paraphrase**. This involves repeating what the other side says.

- I want a 30% discount on all your products
- You want 30% discount on all my products!

Use this to validate a statement made by the other negotiator that seems exaggerated to you, never to underline concessions made by the other negotiator. For example, avoid the following situation:

- I agree to reduce my price by 30% on all my products...
- You agree to reduce your price by 30% on all your products?!
- Uh, no, you're right, maybe that's too much!

Tip #2: **rephrase what the other side says**. It's like paraphrasing, but with different words.

- I want 30% off on all your products

- If I understand correctly, you mean you want me to sacrifice my entire margin to reduce your purchases by 30%?

It's a good way to react when you're not completely sure you understand the person you're talking to. Slide "if I understood correctly" or any variation in this style before rephrasing the person's idea.

Tip #3: **Complete your interviewer's idea** when you feel they are not completing their thinking, with the goal of offering them your solution that they can consider as their own. For example, you could say:

- It's complicated to find two consecutive days of training where everyone is free...
- Would you prefer that we organize the training over two non-consecutive days?

—We have decided to change supplier
—If I understand correctly, you're going to end five years of collaboration without giving us a chance to make a proposal?

—We only work with people we know...
—So if we knew each other, we could work together?
—Yes
—At what point do you consider that you know someone?

Tip #4: **Refocus the discussion** when your interlocutor is very talkative and talks too much. For example, after listening to your interviewer criticize your customer service department for ten minutes, say:

- To sum up, you feel that our after-sales service is not enough to enter into a business relationship, is that right?

This will enable you to avoid entering into a sterile discussion that consists of defending or justifying your after-sales service, argument by argument, because this will not help the negotiation.

Tip #5: if you feel emotions overwhelming your interlocutor, **verbalise** them. For example, if he or she seems angry, tell them:

- I feel you're angry, is there anything in particular I said that you didn't like?

If he seems surprised, say:

- You sound surprised?

This will allow you to get information that would not have been given to you spontaneously.

Encourage the other person to talk, using phrases that will help to reopen the discussion:

- What do you mean?
- Is that so?
- What do you mean by that?

These tips will help you get more information from the other side, especially since you ask open rather than closed questions.

4.8 PERCEPTUAL BIASES DISTORT THE PROPER UNDERSTANDING OF INFORMATION

To negotiate more confidently, you need to analyze the context of the negotiation. This is something that is not really natural, because with so much at stake and so much stress, it is tempting to act as quickly as possible. But with little relevant information, this may lead you to become aggressive or to run away, i.e. accept everything.

So you will have to seek out information. The problem is that it is sometimes difficult to take a step back from this information, and the risk is to misinterpret it, particularly because of the psychological phenomenon of **confirmation bias**.
Confirmation bias consists in retaining only information that confirms what we already think and believe, and leads us to ignore or minimize information that is in contradiction with our beliefs. It is an unconscious phenomenon and that is why it is difficult to avoid it.

You could also be misled by interpretations of reality due to the tendency of everyone to make **hasty generalizations**: it is a phenomenon that consists in giving more importance to the first information received on a subject than to the following ones. For example, you are a supplier to a large company and you enter a meeting for negotiation. You see a pile of documents in a folder labelled "supplier price reductions". You may be inclined to fight over prices in this first meeting, when the issue may be something else, such as delivery delay. But your first impression will influence your ability to listen if you don't pay attention to it.

Biases in the perception of information are not the only pitfalls, one could use an information voluntarily modified or partial, only to have greater leverage in the negotiation later on. But we are dealing with techniques of manipulation of the opposing negotiator that we have already mentioned.

Finally, if you have huge amounts of information to deal with, and it would be impossible for you to deal with it within a reasonable period of time, you could also be led to misunderstand the real situation. For example, the subprime contracts, financial products that led some institutions to fail from 2007 onwards, were complex contracts with interlocking financial products, and the manager of one bank said that understanding subprime in detail was like having to read thousands of pages of documentation. In other words, no one understood anything.

In conclusion, try to be as factual as possible and beware of perception bias. If you are overwhelmed with information, take the time to make it your own and don't decide with your head down.

4.9 SPOTTING THE LIES

In a negotiation, each of the parties hides important elements so that they can use them later in the negotiation. It is difficult to obtain this information, but there are certain elements that make it possible to suspect that your interlocutor is lying.
Obviously, I am not going to make you a specialist in lie detection, so I will focus on elements that are rather easy to spot.
Some clues are to be found in your interviewer's answer, some are to be found in the non-verbal, i.e. in the behavior.

Let's first look at the clues you can find in the other negotiator's speech.

First clue: look for the absence of negation to your question.

- I've been told that your machine hasn't proven to be safe, is that true?
- How can you think that? We've done all the tests.

It's a clue to lying, because the reflex of the person telling the truth is to deny it first. In the case of someone who doesn't lie, the answer is more likely to be:

- But it's not! It is not true! How can you think so, we have done all the tests!

Second clue: instead of answering your question precisely, your interviewer gives you a general answer.

- Have you proven the safety of your machine?
- You know, all machines used for this purpose must have been tested for safety.

Third clue: spot the odd memory loss. Your interviewer responds by adding that he or she has forgotten or doesn't remember it well.

- Have you proven the safety of your machine?
- I don't remember the details, but it seems to me that I have.

Fourth clue: the false question of your interlocutor.

The principle is simple, pretend not to have understood the question. My ten-year-old son does that all the time. I make him recite his multiplication table and when I say 7 x 8, he does it twice out of three times, he answers:

- He says, "What? What multiplication?

The purpose of this question is to get extra time to think. In negotiation, it's the same as with a child: if your interlocutor asks you to reformulate your question when it is simple, clear and the answer should be obvious, it's a sign of lying.

For example, if you ask:

- Have you proven your machine to be safe?

The answer can only be YES or NO and the question is simple. If the person you are talking to hasn't checked the safety of the machine, they may want to lie and give themselves time to think about how they are going to answer. He or she may answer:

- I'm sorry, what? I didn't quite get that.

Or he might...

- You're right to ask that question!

Fifth clue: since it is difficult to lie about complex things, liars tend not to use too many words that are **connectors in sentences**: opposition links ('but', 'unlike', 'however'), cause-and-effect links ('because', 'indeed'). Liars will use evidence markers instead: for example, 'everyone knows that...', 'and' 'moreover' ... These evidence markers imply that you already agree with him and do not require complex thinking.
On the other hand, they will be less likely to say 'I', 'me', 'mine'. This allows them to distance themselves from their lies. If a person talks using the 'I' and then suddenly starts talking using the 'we' or the 'us', it is a sign of lying. For example, suppose someone says the following sentence:
'I'm offering to install our software. You'll see, it's very effective, I guarantee you won't regret it. Moreover, as far as we know, it is the cheapest on the market.'

Saying 'to the best of **our** knowledge' is an indication of a lie, as we go from 'I' to 'we'.

Sixth Clue: Identify large amounts of irrelevant detail not relevant to your question. The person you are talking to is trying to reassure you about something that is not true. For example:

- Have you proven your machine is safe?
- Yes, we started testing on September 5th. And three people from the team were assigned to follow the study of the certification body on a full-time basis between September 6 (they arrived late for the appointment) and September 17. We received the certification on September 25, by mail, which is quite odd, I thought we would get it by email. Did you know that?

The content of the message is not the only one that gives clues about the lie. The non-verbal, i.e. behavior, can also give clues. In principle, the more a person deviates from their usual behavior, the more likely they are to lie.

Seventh clue: Identify changes in voice pitch: If the tone of voice suddenly becomes much higher, it is a clue to lying.

Eighth Clue: if the time taken to answer a simple question to which the answer should be obvious is longer than usual, i.e. there is an oddly long blank, this is a clue to lying.

Detecting lies is not an exact science and you cannot conclude that someone who has one or more of the behaviors described above is lying, but these elements must be signs of vigilance that should lead you to ask additional questions, and possibly to ask for proof for certain statements that you find doubtful.

AUTHOR

Philippe Massol has a doctorate in science and after completing an MBA, worked in an investment fund specialized in innovation. He has been a strategy advisor and now trains both business school students and business professionals on topics related to business development, in particular the quest for new B to B clients.

Philippe Massol is also the French-speaking trainer for LinkedIn Learning for topics related to business development: entrepreneurship, innovation development, sales and customer service.

You can easily reach him on his French LinkedIn account (he speaks English):

https://www.linkedin.com/in/philippemassol/

It could bring value to your company and in particular by training your commercial teams or intrapreneurs.

Printed in Great Britain
by Amazon

58784211R00038